PENINSULA

2023

PENINSULA

PENINSULA

Copyright © 2023 Peninsula

Published in 2023 by Egg Box Publishing, an imprint of UEA Publishing Project, University of East Anglia, Norwich Research Park, Norwich, Norfolk NR4 7TJ

https://www.eggboxpublishing.com/

All rights reserved. This book or any portion thereof may not be reproduced or used in any manner whatsoever without the express permission of the publisher except for the use of brief quotations in a book review or scholarly journal. Contributing writers and artists retain copyright to their works.

Peninsula is typeset in Garamond Premier Pro
Design and typesetting by Harriett Smith
Printed and bound in the UK by Imprint Digital
Distributed by NBN International

ISBN: 978-1-915812-19-3

THE PENINSULA TEAM

General Editor: Ellie Dyer-Brown

Prose Editors: Ed Nickols

Qianying (Ingrid) Liu

Paul Haswell

Poetry Editors: Eden Ward

Elizabeth Marney

Cover Artwork: Izzy Bremner

About the Cover Artwork

The cover artwork is an illustration of a life-size bronze cow statue that looks down the river in Durham towards the Cathedral. It draws inspiration from the legend of the Dun Cow, a story about the journey of a group of Lindisfarne monks moving the body of Saint Cuthbert in 995 AD. During their journey, the coffin came to a halt and would not move. One of the monks had a vision in which Saint Cuthbert appeared and said that the remains should be taken to a place called 'Dunholme', but nobody knew where it was. Then, a milkmaid passed by looking for a dun cow. She encountered a woman who had seen it heading towards Dunholme and pointed out the way. The monks followed the milkmaid, and the coffin started moving again. They followed the road and reached Dunholme (Durham).

Art By: Izzy Bremner

POETRY

Eden Ward

    14   7pm / Lancashire / August

    15   Ode to an evening spent in chatter.

    16   Yet be so young

    17   Tonight

    19   I want to tell you *

Elizabeth Marney

    21   Sometimes when people get married I take it personally

    22   Mercy Killing

    23   Little Religions

    24   Motherless

    26   Whatchamacallit, Thingamajig

    27   One day I will have to address the repercussions of a chaotic youth

Kate Paterson

    28   Simple Phrases

    29   Hush

    30   A Poem as To Why

    32   Nothing, Nothing

Catriona Inglis

    33   Untitled

    35   Border Talk

Nupur Mudgal

    36   The Ballet King

    37   Silly Goose

    38   No Place Like Ours

PROSE

Izzy Bremner

    42 Summer's Stings

Catriona Inglis

    45 The Sunset Crab

Ellie Dyer-Brown

    47 Bluff
    50 Dark Tourism
    53 St. Marks Eve

Paul Haswell

    56 Chicken Living
    58 It's About Time You Got Some Friends Anyway
    62 The Media These Days

Andrea Pinto

    66 One Last Breath
    69 Flame of the Forest

Ed Nickols

    72 Donkey Breath

Matthew Ainley

    80 Pride Pin Badge

POETRY

7pm / Lancashire / August

Not yet sixteen,
Jamie still hasn't gotten sick,
Nobody has died.
It's one of those summer nights
a heavy one
where the sky twists itself
fifteen shades of pink.
The air is hot,
cut with burning wood
and the fleeting rememberings
of how we had grown up here.

We had gotten big,
too old to swing on the willow branches,
so all six of us sat in a circle
eavesdropping
laughter stifled
too young even then
for the dinner table secrets
our parents passed around
with the salt and pepper.

It is our last night on the little table.

I don't see any empty cans
when I look back
the table is laid only with hot food
flamed fresh from the barbecue.
Grandad laughs,
fat-bellied and rosy
not yet heart scared slim.
I lean on arms that would
never find their way around me again.
our faces are so round
our hair terribly long —
neither cut into adulthood's knife.

My mother is still one of four,
and there is so much life yet to come.

Ode to an evening spent in chatter.

Is there not some art
to this act of nothing?
Sitting in low light
meandering
along soft conversation —
Like a leaf resting
on its glassy river
I float through
these words.
It is easy here.
There is such wonder
in watching the thought
as it glitters
in the deep
of your iris
before its shape
can find your lips.

I delight in you with a type
of glee I feared had been
surrendered to childhood;
There is our laughter,
rich and throaty and warm
woven through our
talkings of god and art.
When darkness falls
the cold stays sitting
at the doorstep —
The night that
creeps in is nearly balmy.

On a lilting eve
like the one which
has caught us,
I think I must be joy splattered.

Yet be so young

I want to carve
the memory of this

                        cut it evenly like
                  a slice of supermarket

                                      tray bake I'll wrap
                                    carefully in a pink

napkin store it in
my pocket for the

                      walk as years lilt
                      on I will find

                                    crumbs now half woven
                                      into the coat lining

catching under nail forgotten
and persistent I remember

                    how sweet it tasted
                    to feel so old,

                                        yet be so young.

Tonight

i am nightmare sick
in a cold bed
my ribs splinter under this
twilight spectres palm
the grip winds
sharp and boundless
down into my jugular

like fidgeting maggots
a choking fear burrows
into my cadaver eyes
dusk's terror rots
into my skull and
wrenches sleepless teeth
from these aching gums

shadows haunt my bedside
whisper a yellow sickness
into my burning wheeze
tall and watching they
seize my ankles while the
salt beads pool,
scorching an open gash
across my burning neck

i fight for consciousness
swimming against
the dark and murky waters
i find my head held under
my lips sleep sewen
hoarse pleas
crumbled to ruin

tonight I am fear doused
afraid of sleep
afraid of what viciousness
lurks behind that half-cracked
wardrobe door

bared teeth and a vulture lust for
my fitting malady
i am parasite ridden and terrified
i battle the weight
of my leaded eyelids.
fear drags me under.
the last dregs of awakeness
succumb to this grotesqueness
in sleep my corpse
will be picked over.

I want to tell you *

—

I open my eyes
whilst yours lay still closed
on another of those mornings
where you have sheltered in my sheets.

In the haze of the night just passed
under curls of street-lit fog,
our lips can-frozen blue,
we raced arm in arm.

Our fingers wound
locked tightly in a pinkie promise,
two cracked voices bouncing
echoed back to us from above:

"YOU ARE YOUNGER
THAN EVERY STAR
PEERING DOWN
FROM THE SKY!"

Night-soaked we tumbled
over the rain-licked cobbles
skinning our knees
blowing our smoke,

chattering past the swimming pool
and riverbank
past the car parks
and through the cathedrals bell —

1 it tolls
2 again
3 your eyes widen
4 is it really so late?

When we collapse into sleep.
I want to tell you *

I want to pry your eyes open
and make sure you know *

I'd stamp it onto your shoulders,
with pen ink and a safety pin,
scratch it with my fingernails
into the palm of your hand...

* YOU
ARE
MY VERY
BEST FRIEND

Sometimes when people get married I take it personally

I was accused of being quietly dramatic once.
I like to think of it like that time Lord Byron dressed his pillow in his clothes and launched it from a second storey window just to see if his family would care if he died, apart from instead of doing that I just think about whether my friends hate me a little bit too often and
make big life decisions based on the chance
of laughing about it later.
My friends must get terrible second hand
embarrassment from me.

A man once told me that if I was thinner and blonder I'd be the type of person to blow kisses at people and call it a personality trait and I'm still not really sure what he meant by that. That was nowhere near as bad, though, as the time a man told me I'm the type of girl you
marry, not fuck and I laughed and felt very
bad because I did not want to get married,
I wanted to fuck.
Once I asked my mother why I am the way that I am when I could literally not do that.
She told me that some people are just addicted to being who they are.
Now I'd call that dramatic.

Mercy Killing

On the last day of Summer
we stood at a barbecue
charring sweetcorn and
peppers as a bumblebee,
dazed, dropped onto the grill.
She seemed so soft
even as she melted
— I burned my fingers
trying to peel her away.
I'm not sure you can tell
when an insect is in pain
but she must have been
so I placed her on the grass
so softly. You saw her and
stomped her back into mud.
I asked you what it felt like.
Doesn't everything have to
feel like something else?

Little Religions

He spends the summer of '18 in Italy.
Returns with a tattoo of a cross,
cradled in the crook of his arm.
We argue about God until he cries.

*Do you remember being
seven years old?
The boys in the field who called me a bitch?
You: this little bundle
of fury, headfirst into the fight.
They beat the shit out of you.*

*You didn't regret it.
You laughed, as we walked back home:
'It's just a black eye, Giorgi,
some things are more important
than a bruise.'*

*I told my mother I hated you, that night.
And then I went to bed,
prayed I'd know you forever.*

Motherless

Mother leafs through
photos of the life she
lead without her, her
breath catching in her
throat, garbled and
choked as if tobacco
stained fingers still
dig into her neck.
She realises, now,
that her absence
was never felt.

I never graduated to
being an afterthought,
she muses, cross-legged
on the bedroom floor,
let alone a consideration.

What a task for the
people she loved the
least, to rifle through
her belongings, chuck
her shit into bin bags.
Build an idea of a
stranger whose body lay
cold, here, days before.
I tell my mother the
photographs are of
little use to me now.
If I wanted a part of Irene
I'd frame one of the empty
bottles from the floor.

Mother laughs, deflated.

Irene, the two days
a year liquor did not
soften your day
were when I did

instead, trundling up
grey staircases to
your council flat
in the towers.
Reaching for shaking
hands to pull me
in for a hug.
We never doubted
you loved me,
Irene, in those
thirty two days,
in the sixty four
hours of my life
you borrowed on
momentary sobriety.

I have wiped my mother's tears since before
I understood sadness.
Did you realise, Irene, what you had done?

Whatchamacallit, Thingamajig

(one)
appendage

inflated sac

decalibrated erogenous
        territory

hit me...
                ...I dare you

a girl!

                                      (two)
                              curious pig
                     mouth stuffed with...

                                do not touch!

                                    but look
                      please
             beg
              bitch
                            this is no heaven
          I'm just dying?

(three)
rabbit brained man

pornography
        educated
                (derogatory
                      tone)
sticky with sweat
and...

remember
        who I am
                a person
(please)

One day I will have to address the repercussions of a chaotic youth

The last time I argued with a man he told me
I am not mean, I do not know how to be.
When I am mad my words blur and
hiss like an out of tune radio.

I picture you sometimes
with your legs pinned in the air
just for me
and a halo on your head.

I could not fall from grace if I tried.

I could stand you more if you were meaner.

He tells me that I only know how to be vulnerable
when the stakes are low...

It's a flaw, it's a big fucking flaw

but I am still the coolest girl he has ever met.
I am there when he calls, I am there when he wants me.
A good girl like that will leave a man in ruin —
he is crying because he is in love with me.
He never wants to see me again.

I say I've been messy, real messy,
coke habit for the aesthetic messy
disappear for weeks messy
fuck your best friend messy.
I'm not sorry. Not one bit.
Where's my halo now...

It's on your head.
It's where it always has been.
I'll forgive you,
I always forgive you.

I want to scream

my mistakes belong to me —
give them back.

Simple Phrases

Lights blur through the car window
tears of rain racing each other
even though silence fills the stands.
The drum of his fingers on the steering wheel
creates a beat to the unspoken words

> *Don't be ridiculous, she is not going to judge us.*

It's her job to judge us. That's why you are paying her.

> *Why are you pinning this on me?*

*You just want her to tell you why you are completely
right and what is wrong with me.*

> *That is not true.*

Simple phrases leave us in ruin,
more so than the untold futures
where any movement
or tone inflection
would be judged

Whatever.

> *God, you can be such an asshole.*

Echoes from their earlier meeting
playing through their minds
where one played with their broken cuticles
allowing for the other to speak for them.
The other voiced how neither wanted to be there.

Hush

Silence holds the most words, and we could have written a novel. I think back to that night, where the silence had told us that what we had was over. It wasn't the verbal daggers or the glacier of moments which explained our failures. Instead, it was the silence in the air, as the gravity of what you had said held between us.

A Poem as To Why

Golden rays danced over your bare skin.
The red light from the clock
ticking down the time until your train.
If I didn't say it now, I never would.
Like a movie you stood,
hair whipping,
eyes watering,
a summer romance dying

until it wasn't.
A few months later we bumped into each other
somewhere along Edinburgh's Royal Mile.
In mid-winter you were wrapped up in cotton.
Dragon's breath floating into the sky
as you drank the hot chocolate I bought for you.
You always say this moment was where we began,
I always thought it was that first night on the beach.

It just made sense for us to move in with each other,
where our leases ended,
where we spent two years together,
where we couldn't wait to see the other after the end of the day.
Our lives and possessions were coming together.
We didn't even need to talk about who got which side of the bed.
I always thought that life would resemble how we felt in that cramped apartment.

As quickly as it started
the day finished with you dressed in white lace
our families finally intertwined.

In retrospective hindsight,
and involuntary couples counselling,
I've come to realise why you reacted that way.

You reacted well. At first.
But when the reality set in on what this meant for you,
what this meant for us,

comments which were once sweet
became vile and malicious.

We both kept things bottled away
until the worst points.
Where we began to unravel
with the liquor that painted our lips.
We went to bed that night
back-to-back,
but an ocean of pain between us.

Night calls for home, waiting for a response.

Nothing, Nothing

We said goodbye at the door,
you held your car keys and purse in your hands.

We hugged without saying goodbye,
you stumbled over your words.

We found this decision was for the best,
you were the one who wanted to move out.

We decided it was best to have a break,
you wholeheartedly agreed.

We don't know when we will next see each other again,
you didn't want a time frame.

I turned on the TV, anticipating your voice.

I didn't know which channel to pick.

I hoped a shower may help to wash your smell from my body.

I went to bed wanting to hold you.

I lay staring at the ceiling and found that sleep had finally settled.

Untitled

'but when you have to turn into a chrysalis —
you will someday, you know'
— *Lewis Carroll Alice's Adventures in Wonderland*

I'm not myself when I'm with you
The way my face creases
At your laughter
Is unknown to me
I did not dream of smiles like these
Of days that run long
Into yearning.

I am not myself
I do not taste of strawberries
         Of summer
Of decadence like I have joy to
Spare, to overflow
I do not hold favours like trophies
I do not choose deliverance.

I cannot catch dragonflies
If I held the moment of you
It would fall away into dust
Return and return again to the
Curve of your hip
That gives grace like it is owed
To teach me the crease of your elbow.

I am not this other
When I am with you
I leave this self-severing
To renumeration that I pledge will never come.
My self is old cotton
Holed by loving fingers
This self is a self of fine silk.

I am with you
And it is like I have left herself behind

Left to play old games.
Score a canyon between us
Cast her to an abyss of black holes
Melt from it some new star
That alights free from frost.
Left to play old games.
Score a canyon between us
Cast her to an abyss of black holes
Melt from it some new star
That alights free from frost.
I am not myself when I am with you
I have not my self
With you I take each breath as mine.
When I am with you
I know what it is to be so
Me
other self

Border Talk

I cannae mind seagulls
    — Sea Eagles
South doone as far as Dumfries
Fish supper in fancy boxes
A havoc of clitter clatter
The cutlery shuffles

It's no cashmere
Cashmere, no, you can ken from the thread count
Dishes cleared to clacker on next door
It was hard then, you ken, no helmets then
Back when shinty wa' a real sport

They might get marry they might not
So dinnie rush and get your heart out
The cluster of dropped consonants
has a remembrance of childhoods.

They gave ye a license wi' that photo?
Goodness gracious me!
Pitch and eyebrow jockey for height
As the photo passes from laugh to cackle

Who's daft and who's right?
Leave with pictures of the riding
Souters regaled in rosettes and flag
    I cannae Ken hae many evenings pass so
But I know they do pass.

The Ballet King

The reason I tell you this story is so obvious; you have nothing better to do and neither do I!
The night after his coronation, he has a drink or two, blows his nose on his satin robe & cries as he missed his ballet class. 'Stupid crown, stupid crown'! he shouts to no one in particular.
Oh, the twist & twirl in the room he loves. Etendre. Sauter. Glancerand elance!
He moves around the room with elegance and modesty. No, no! He stops midway, a king doesn't
dance, he rules. Arrogant, haughty, brave — these are a good king's traits.
His mind is engaged in an ineffable contemplation
to get rid of, to get rid of, oh he can't speak it out loud, to get rid of the crown!
He'll be a lousy ruler for sure, then they won't burden him with the crown.
He set his plan in motion the next day, busting with adrenaline.
All day he sits on his throne staring at his royal crew. One has a chapped nose; one keeps on adjusting his trousers, one is eyeing a female servant and the other never stops talking! Idiots!
He sits and sits and sits and sits, never bothering to give an opinion — and that's what makes a nasty king! In fact, he is the worst king that ever ruled the lands of Windford. From Sherryl town to Transter State estrange babble spread like wildfire, of a king whose manners and appearance did not reckon to please. He scowls and snores all day long and rushes out of the halls after the day's crip and crap. Then the horrible king's day really begin, he sneaks out of his room when everyone is inbed and asleep and creeps into the quite basement. He intently listens to any noise from up above
and yet after close consideration there was no sound heard. He then practices his flowing movements, bursting with energy and happiness he keeps on twirling. There never was a king so graceful and pleasant. He dances without winking and at the end gives a great leap! You are bound to admit that he is made to dance and not to rule but you can leave all that to themighty king — he has big plans to disappoint everyone around!
You may meet him at the border of the town, you may see him on his toes — But when they appoint someone new for the crown, he'll never again be there!

Silly Goose

Silly goose liked to gossip, with friends and enemies alike:
In fact, he had an extensive reputation for knowing everything.
At the break of dawn, he'd visit all his mischievous neighbors
for a cup of tea, bagels, and sometimes a piece of cake.
But most of all... for a whisper of their notorious doings,
sometimes he wouldn't get any tittle-tattle for a week or two,
he'd roam around dejectedly, preening his feathers, and
scoffing at everyone he meets — aggressive, I tell you!
However gradually the air was filled with scandalous chatter
and the silly, silly, our very silly goose was delighted again.

If that extrovert duck ran away with the gorgeous turkey
and the mama duck is a mess — won't stop sobbing,
If the accounts of the Big Swan's grocery shop aren't right,
despite multiple attempts to match the math... poor Swan,
If the fellow geese family has started quarrelling again,
over who hid the TV remote, who finished the ice cream,
or who sneaked out late at night for a goose's dance party:
Then the whole society would say — "Call that silly goose!
He has a very unusual gift of being a know-it-all."
And then the remarkably smart but silly goose would
adjust his red tie and come forward with much suavity.
He'd spill all the secrets... one after another, there you go.
And the folks would say: "Well, no that can't be...but it makes sense...
Really...Oh no... How could they?... sounds about right...
Just like that the silly, silly, our very silly goose was delighted again.

No Place Like Ours

Did I tell you that there is a stranger on the train
who reminds me too much of her bloody red hair.

Did I tell you that she sits naked on the bedroom floor
peeling an avocado to plant a tree in the living room.
Green spills all over her legs and the corners of her dry lips.
She pauses. Stares at the beautifully cut fruit and squeezes it
over the bruised wooden tiles.
Her frozen stare pervades the wretchedness of the place,
the place we once called home. Ours.
I am not making up any of this, in my head she is still smiling,
her lips are not parched, not yet —
they are the color of the sunset,
the agony of her soul has not yet reached her organs.
Not yet. Not yet.
But the wine glass beside her pale thighs will tell you otherwise.
Her bleeding hands will narrate the sinking truth.

Did I tell you that she has stopped listening
to my screams, my aching heart.
So, I whisper love in her ears —
I feel the need to keep her from falling!
But it's too late, she is already someone else
or she has gone back to herself.

PROSE

Summer's Sting

Somehow, they are acting out this scene again. Or perhaps this precise variation hasn't happened before, he couldn't say. Three strands of blonde hair caught against a cheek in the sunlight. Her arm, stained eggshell-brown from the sun, stretching towards the fruit bowl in the middle of the table, the orange that she takes looking down at its own crude portrait on the plastic tablecloth. The ebb and flow of the floor-length skirt as it moves towards the sink — the orange has left a sticky residue on her skin, but wasn't it sweet and huge? The thin golden line that traces her movements like a sparkler where the sun hits the tiny fibres on her clothes.

If he closes his eyes, this outline is imprinted on his eyelids, blinding against the blackness. The scent of the orange lingers in the air, tart and stringy on the thick, soft afternoon breeze that ambles in through the open double doors. Sunlight is thrown across the room in a patchwork through each small square of glass, and trickles like honey down the cream kitchen walls. All of a sudden, he is tired.

'It's the market tomorrow.' She presses play on an old CD player and soft guitar plucks the air. 'I think I'll walk into town, if you want to come. I want to pick up some more incense sticks to freshen the place up before we leave.'

He thought it seemed fresh enough. He doesn't say this out loud, though.

She tries again.

'We need some more bread to get us through the last couple of days, too. Shall I get some cheese?'

'There's some brie in the fridge. And some Mont d'Or. That'll be enough.'

'Ah. That's fine, then.' The silence is sticky, and the music works hard to pull it apart. The river glugs at the end of the garden, and birds whistle idly from its banks. She shoots him tentative glances and he pretends not to notice. He is sitting parallel to the table with his head propped on his hand, the curve of his neck bared over the collar of his blue linen shirt as he turns the page of his book. She knows he's only pretending to read it. He knows that she knows this. They've been playing this game for a while now.

He doesn't take his eyes off the page as she walks up behind him, and his muscles tense slightly as her hands come to rest on his shoulders. She strokes them up and down his arms and brings her chin to rest in the crook of his neck. Skin on skin, the rules of the game don't apply. He closes his eyes and lets his head relax against hers, bringing his thumb up to graze her cheek softly. These moments feel like blossom or butterfly wings, natural, beautiful. Try too hard to hold them and they'll break. She smells yellow and blue, and he is powerless against it. He breathes out heavily, and their breath intertwines on the air. Nothing moves. Summer tripped and fell at their feet and these final, heavy days won't seem to budge. And so, they are stuck, and June is July is August, and the air between them is thick and awkward and harder to breathe than it was at the beginning. Still, when she touches him, he forgets this, and he's sure that she forgets it too, and each point of contact is a spark or a drop of molten gold. Yet, afterwards, the negative space where their bodies have been seems emptier each time. In seconds, the spell is broken and she stands up straight again, and his neck burns where her skin has been. She picks up a mug of ginger tea from the counter — surely cold by now — and drifts silently into the garden. She stops at the easel that she has religiously taken out onto the lawn every morning of the summer, and stares once again at the empty canvas. Part of him wants to scream at her in frustration — why does she bother? — but he has neither the will nor the energy to muster such passion.

This thought is gently interrupted by the gleeful yells of a boatful of children on the river drifting up the lawn, the unskilled splash of oars punctuating each line. He watches her as she contemplates the sound from the grass. Spending the summer at his parents' house on the Dordogne was supposed to have helped them move on, yet each day that they spend stewing in each other's shadow, the pain simply swells and heaves.

Three more nights. Three more nights, and they'll be back in Edinburgh, and they can go about their lives pretending that nothing happened and nothing has changed. The act still needs polishing, though. It has rusted under summer's sweat and tears.

—

The next morning, the road into town is dusty, and the air is thick with pollen and last night's dew. In this part of France, you can usually rely on the rain to quench the heaviness once in a while, but this summer has been hot, and the land is bitter about it. The toe of an espadrille scratches the sandy tarmac. She adjusts the canvas shopping bag as it slides feebly from her shoulder. He clears his throat, and she looks at him hopefully, but nothing follows.

The house is only a ten-minute walk from town, and cars rarely come this way, anyway; only a couple of farmhouses sit neatly in the surrounding fields, and his parents' villa sits among a handful of ancient, elegant buildings — mostly second homes, now — that are balanced at varying intervals along the rim of the river. Otherwise, this road is a dead end.

Soon, they're swaddled in the hum of the honey-coloured market town and twist themselves deeper into the cobbled streets until they're buried in the centre. Bread and incense and cheese and leather and smoke and dried meats and a hundred herbs instantly smother him. He can't breathe. Someone waves at them from across the square; it is the woman who owns the café on the corner. Even from here, he can see the pity behind her smile.

Back in June, when they first arrived, she had served them each a coffee and started asking questions. He's been here almost every summer since he was born, so of course she recognised him, and his father had always been on good terms with the locals. Back again? Please, have this one on the house, my treat. But where's the little one?

The gaping silence that followed still rings in his ears two months later.

Now, he politely raises a hand in greeting, then averts his gaze as his eyes begin to prickle. He feels that he might melt into the cobbles and be ground into the dirt under the sandals of the tourists and frustrated locals that buzz past. As he drops his hand back to his side, he finds it impulsively reaching for hers.

She doesn't let herself react as their fingers interlock, lest he should change his mind and take them back.

The Sunset Crab

It was on a Wednesday evening, the first Wednesday of the first November after the incident, on a beach just five miles from St David's that, whilst taking in the way the orange of the winter sunset reflected in ripples on the cold surface of the sea, I first met the crab. I've met the crab just two times since. Once was on a rainy and particularly miserable Thursday eight months after the initial meeting where the crab simply asked me, 'do you remember what I told you on our first meeting?', and I told it that I did remember and that was the end of it. The subsequent meeting was exactly three months later when the crab came across to me in a state of acute distress and said that I'd done as it had said and that I'd not be seeing it again.

 You told me once that there is a special type of magic in watching sunsets. You told me, after watching a particularly spectacular one and seeing the sharp colours that you had forgotten existed in your conventionally grey life, that those colours could be pressed into the empty spaces of greyscale between the bones of your ribcage instead of being pushed away by the darkening night. It was for that reason that watching sunsets could remind you how to hope again. And perhaps that is why I came to watch the sunset that day on the first Wednesday of the first November after the incident, the day that would've been our anniversary, and perhaps that is why my request for hope was answered by the crab.

 I didn't notice it at first but then it spoke, and the voice was softer than I would've expected. It asked where you were. I told it that you had died and then, assuming that you and the crab had been friends of a sort, I offered my condolences. I remember that felt strange at the time, like playing the wrong part in a show you had rehearsed. For months I had been the receiver rather than the giver of condolences; I found I rather liked the change. Crabs cannot smile but I imagine if they could, the crab would've smiled at me then, as if it knew that I liked this opportunity to share a piece of my grief by offering it as sympathy to another living thing.

 We watched the moon rise above the silent ocean together. There was no one else on the beach that day to see the tears we both shed for you. As our tears dried, as the saltwater drained in soft streams along the sand to meet the sea, the crab turned to me. It didn't ask how you died. I assumed that it already knew, as it had the feeling of a creature who knew most things without needing to ask. But I wonder now if it just didn't feel it would've helped me to have to return to my usual role as receiver of condolences by recollecting again in agonising remembrance the instances of your death. It was right of course. Instead, it asked again where you were. I wondered if it was mirroring my own denial of your departure or if crabs had memories akin to that of goldfish and simply didn't remember; I could relate to that too: in the long nightmares of my dreams I forgot and remembered anew and each time the remembering took more colour out of my life. So, I told it again that you had died. 'That is not where you are,' it said of you, 'that it is where you are not'. I told it that in that case I didn't know where you were; that I was not the theistic sort and had, prior to your death, not spent much time contemplating the metaphysical implications of an after-world; and that since your death I found that, though I now dwelt on it often, I could come to no such conclusions.

The crab gave me the sort of look you used to give me when I had said something particularly stupid, and you were waiting for me to notice. The crab told me to leave the metaphysics and that I needed to go and find you in the places I remembered you. Then it left and I was alone on the cold beach breathing warm air into my gloveless hand.

It took me several months to find you. I didn't see the crab in that time though I often returned to that beach hoping to speak to it again, to ask it if it knew where you were. I looked for you in all our old haunts: in all the rooms of your house, now transformed into someone else's; in the sugared icing of our favourite bakes, somehow tasteless without your solid presence; on the stage of the theatre you used to love; I even wandered the grimy streets of the path between our houses as if I'd turn a corner and find you there. But I didn't find you. Each place opened a new shattering inside me, our secret places remained unlit without the brilliance of your smile. It took me eleven months, but, on the third Thursday of the second October after the incident, I found you. I should've known you would be here.

Bluff

It was around the summer of my thirteenth birthday — when the sun-soaked days stretched into night, and my friends and I would pedal through the twilight, ditching our bikes on the pavement near Mrs Barker's house — that the butcher's shop opened in our small, dozy village. Rumours circled around the shop (as they do all new things), sparked chiefly by us boys, who liked to imagine each missing pet, each death, had somehow occurred at the hands of the butcher, who contrived such misfortunate events to steal the bodies and sell the cuts in his shop.

Our village, Bluff, left little opportunity for amusement for its children. There were a handful of houses, pebble-dashed and squat, and not much to do except cause trouble, which — I'm ashamed to admit — we regularly did. Knock-a-door-run was our favourite game, and Mrs Barker, with her peculiar, stooped posture and her gnarled fingers, was our preferred target.

We told each other she was a witch or sometimes a vampire (how else to explain her jet-black hair that had survived almost eight decades when the rest of her body had deteriorated so naturally?), and the story changed from week to week. It was a competition, you see, among proud young boys, to see who could conjure up the scariest tale and who, in response, would prove himself the faintest of heart. It helped our imaginations that Mrs Barker was the most fervent — often the only — customer of the butcher, returning home with (we imagined) dripping packages of meat parcelled up in brown paper.

On one humid August evening, it was my turn to kick off our wicked game. We abandoned our bikes by the curb, and the others crept forward, ghost-white in the failing light, tucking themselves out of view behind the garden wall.

I strode up the path, buoyed by the confidence of a long-reigning champion. Perhaps if I had possessed a modicum of self-doubt, I would have seen the twitch of the net curtains, and if I had paused before knocking, I would have heard dragging footsteps behind the door. As it was, I did not apprehend either of these signs that the usual course of our game was about to be disrupted.

My knuckles had barely grazed the wood when I heard the bolt unfastening. To explain the abject horror I felt as four crooked fingers appeared around the edge of the door is impossible, even to this day. I only know that the gasps of my friends sank me deeper into despair.

I tried to turn and run, but — too late. One of those hands latched onto my shoulder, and I turned slowly to stare Mrs Barker in the eyes, thinking I would show my friends, whom I realised were watching from a distance, that I was not afraid.

Only, when I turned, the sight that met my eyes was hardly what I expected: not the glistening fangs of a vampire ready to puncture my neck, but an old woman clutching her chest, rheumy eyes wide with fear, mouth gaping in a silent 'o'. I recognised the symptoms instantly — my father had gone the same way; he'd always said his dodgy ticker would take him, in the end — and, spurred to action, I called to my friends: 'Phone an ambulance!'

Mrs Barker's skin was the colour of ash, and a horrible rasping sound was coming from her pale lips. The fear in her eyes, most of all, was what made me act. I grasped her shoulders, leading her to the wooden bench beside the front door, trying to remember what I'd learnt from the medical book I borrowed from the library after my father went.

'Aspirin!' I said. 'Do you have any aspirin?'

She was beyond words.

'Call an ambulance!' I shouted again to my friends. This time, they scattered, sprinting up the road to the nearest phone box as Mrs Barker clutched her linen night dress. I realised there was nothing for it; I'd have to go inside.

I had never thought, not even for a moment, I would enter this house and see the inner workings of the old woman's life: the grandfather clock looming in the hallway, ticking the same second over and over, blanketed in dust, or the peeling, faded linoleum in the kitchen, sticky under my feet. On a shelf above the sink, a collection of ceramic owls watched me as I pulled open drawers, rummaging amongst mismatched cutlery and bric-a-brac, running my hand along the top of the fridge in the hope of finding a medicine box. The pads of my fingers came away coated with a thick layer of dirt that I hastily wiped on my jeans, feeling nauseous.

Hearing sirens in the distance, I turned to go, but not before I saw on the sink in the downstairs bathroom, visible only because the door had been left ajar, a bottle of jet-black hair dye.

My friends fled before the ambulance arrived, but I rode with Mrs Barker to the hospital, watching with horror as the paramedics tried to shock her body to life, attempting to answer questions about who she was and all kinds of things the grandson that I said I was should have known.

She drifted in and out of consciousness as the paramedics wheeled her out of the ambulance and through the doors of the hospital, her puckered mouth moving noiselessly. The soles of my trainers slapped against the sterile vinyl floor as I jogged beside the gurney, losing momentum. Whatever adrenaline had brought me here was rapidly fading, and my limbs, no longer electrified, felt heavy as lead.

There was a moment of stillness as the paramedics and doctors shared a quick, hushed briefing in the corridor. Mrs Barker was looking horribly pale. She stretched a thin arm out, gesturing for me to come closer. Despite myself, I still felt a thrill of fear as I approached. Her eyes were unfocused, rolling around as if in search of something. She waited until I was close enough to feel her warm, sweet breath against my cheek — close enough to notice the thin line of grey at the roots of her hair — before she whispered in one last breath, 'don't let the butcher have me.'

Dark Tourism

It has been a day of receiving phone calls enquiring about the location of Bluff's public car park (there isn't one) and whether Windy Hill has wheelchair access (it doesn't). Clare puts her head in her hands; being head of the Tourism Board for a town like this is no easy job. She has already written her letter of resignation just in case the events of the evening go awry.

You'd think Bluff's infamous witch hunt of 1643 would be enough to attract curious outsiders. For a time, it was. A descendant of one of the witches, Miriam Hubbard (not her real surname; Clare is sworn to secrecy), used to take tour groups up to the site before people stopped visiting. Until today, the commemorative plaque on Windy Hill had been forgotten by all but the most devoted of residents — just another root in the twisted tree of the village's history. Miriam will be pleased to reprise her role, delivering the guests to the evening's festivities at precisely the right time.

If they don't attract enough visitors, it's over. For Clare and the town. The energy of a place like Bluff can only last for so long without being replenished, and you can hardly be Head of Tourism for a town that doesn't exist, can you?

She packs her bag — a flask of tea and shortbread biscuits, a radio for communicating with Miriam, a canister of Zippo fluid — and stomps across the frozen fields by torchlight to Windy Hill. Even before she reaches the top, Clare can see the outline of the towering pyre her swarm of volunteers has been erecting all week: broken drawers sawn into pieces, smashed crates, an old writing bureau she recognises from the village hall. Pieces of Bluff sacrificed for the cause.

Clare squints up at the sky but sees no stars; Mrs. Taylor's prophecy of snow (unsolicited, meted out during one of her lengthy calls to the Tourism Board about her latest visions) looks more and more likely. Winter has settled over Bluff early this year; she worries, in this cold snap, whether her plans will even be possible.

'Is that wood wet?' Clare calls.

'Clare?' Patrick's head torch flashes, momentarily blinding her.

'I specifically said no damp wood. You have to think about the smoke. And the smell, how it will carry...' She tries to keep the panic out of her voice, thinking about the residents of Goathland, a village two miles east, who kicked up a stink about the noise during Bluff's summer solstice festival. It will be fine. This is fine.

'It's only a bit of damp,' says Patrick. 'We'll light the middle first, where the dry stuff is at the bottom, and by the time that's burning — '

'Quiet,' Clare interrupts, holding a hand up to silence her colleague.

The more she shines her torch through the darkness — hazy, now, as tendrils of mist roll up the hill — the more her anxiety boils over into a simmering, then churning, anger. The light of her torch catches someone slinging a pine branch — feathered with green needles — to the top of the pile. The children of Bluff have emerged from their homes, dragging logs and branches out of the woods to the south. They will be wet, the lot of them, not fit to burn, and probably rotten, too.

'No wet wood!' Clare shouts, but it's pointless; her voice is lost to their thrilled screams. She turns to Patrick. 'Have you heard anything from the Inn?'

'Aye,' he huffs. 'Full house. Jim says he's had to put some of them in the basement. More people than he knows what to do with, he says!'

At least something has gone to plan. But what to do with them if the fire won't light? She checks her watch. Thirty minutes to the witching hour. Thirty minutes until, on this day, at this time three hundred and fifty years ago, fifteen women were burnt at the stake.

Claire slings her backpack to the ground and pulls out the Zippo canister. It is a tiny amount of fluid, she realises, compared to the grand scale of the pyre, but she douses it on the wood anyway. She has worked too hard for this to fail.

'Light the fire.'

'You're sure?'

'Do it.'

Clare steps back, along with the volunteers and children, and Patrick pulls a small box from his pocket. She is doubtful, watching him give it a shake — for good luck — and slip a single match from its dark bed. The feeling lasts only a moment before she discards it. On top of Windy Hill, all is silent.

Patrick strikes the match.

The residents of Bluff hold their breath, transfixed as the tiny flaming stick finds its way into the heart of the pyre, where it glows and flickers but does not catch. It waits.

Clare takes a deep breath and imagines it: the gasoline-soaked wood ignites, sending a wall of heat into their faces so fierce that several people stumble back. Not Clare: she tips her chin up, closes her eyes, relishes the burn. What would it have been like for those women hundreds of years ago, bound to a stake as the flames licked at their melting skin? Would the air in Bluff have changed, electrified? Would the women have felt, while the flames devoured them, the earth growing stronger beneath their feet, as Clare does now? She imagines the scent of singed hair and burning bodies curdling in the air. The screams, then the silence, of the women.

Not witches, not really — not to anyone who knew. It was a small sacrifice.

Clare's radio crackles to life. Are you ready for us?

'Yes,' she says, to both the radio and the match. 'We're ready.'

At the bottom of Windy Hill, the tourists begin their ascent.

—

Two weeks later, Clare finds Miriam in her office, holding a copy of the *Yorkshire Enquirer*. She takes the newspaper and scans the front-page headline: Missing Tourists After Bluff Witch Trials Anniversary.

Clare smiles. The police arrived last week with their questions and theories, though they quickly realised the people of Bluff are naturally suspicious of outsiders and unlikely to respond with more than a grunt or a heckle. After a brief round of interrogations, they spent most of their time up Windy Hill, which they cordoned off while they searched for evidence of a fire. When questioned, people from Goathland apparently swore they had smelled smoke — that it wafted, thick and dark, across the moors. But upon inspection, the police found that the ground on top of the hill, blanketed with lush grass and a healthy crop of inkcap mushrooms, bore no scar. Although they started excavating (much to the dismay of Bluff's foraging society), they quickly gave up on that line of enquiry, finding nothing other than an unusually large population of earthworms.

Since then, the Tourism Board's telephone has been ringing off the hook. Clare is told the village has become a hotspot for dark tourism, whatever that means. It has been described, in some alternative publications, as the new Bermuda triangle.

She thinks: let them come.

St. Mark's Eve

My mother, who had come prepared with blankets, mushroom tea and a fistful of sage, moved the small silver cross on her necklace from side to side, sensing a shift in the graveyard. The church bell tolled; it was an hour before midnight. Frost had begun to gather around the mossy gravestones, glittering faintly as it crept towards us, disturbing the mild April air. I held my breath when it reached the stone wall where we were sitting, on the boundary of the church grounds. According to my mother, it could reach no further. *Don't be scared*, she had said when we arrived, *there's nothing to fear.*

Now, her eyes had a kind of emptiness, wide and glassy, fixed on a point near the church. I followed her gaze. 'What can you see?'

'Quiet,' she whispered. 'Drink your tea, Maria.'

Like a good child, I raised the cup to my lips, preparing for the bitter, earthy taste and nausea that would follow. This was my mother's ritual — her duty carried out for the people of Bluff — but never before had she allowed me to accompany her, much less share her tea.

'Christopher Merton.' A breeze of ice-cold air blew through my hair as my mother's voice broke the silence. I stared hard at the porch - the grand wooden door left open, beckoning — but I saw nothing.

I scribbled the name down in my notebook. It was familiar; of course it was. Everybody knew everybody in a place like Bluff. I had spent the past week wandering around the town in a daze, feeling the tar of dread solidifying in my mouth each time I encountered a friend or relative. How could I speak to these people normally when I might be responsible for recording their impending death?

'Rebecca Tobyn.'

Another name in the notebook. My handwriting was barely legible: a spidery scrawl at the mercy of my cold shivers.

'Jonathan Clarke.'

The bouncing letters on the page grew and shrank. Tree branches on the periphery of my vision transformed into dark figures standing watchfully over the graves; everywhere I looked, there was a strange shape, a darkness that needed accounting for, just out of my sight.

'Charlie Petter.'

The nausea that had been building in my stomach became urgent. I retched, partly because of the tea, partly because I had thought, for a second, that the name announced was the one I didn't want to hear. Charlie Blackwood, my little brother.

It occurred to me, as I watched the frost dancing in strange patterns, that perhaps my mother hadn't brought me here because of my endless nagging, nor because she thought I was finally old enough. After all, what was the difference, really, between sixteen and seventeen? Perhaps she had brought me here for her. Just in case one of the souls wandering through this graveyard on St Mark's Eve was his.

'Promise you'll tell me, Maria.' Charlie fixed his eyes firmly on mine as the nurse slid a needle into his forearm, drawing blood. It was a simple enough process that he'd experienced a hundred times, but it still made him nervous. 'I want to know.'

'But I don't want to know. I can't bear the thought of...'

Those words hung in the air before me. The words I could never say; that none of us, except for Charlie, could ever say. He always seemed so at ease with the idea of his own death. Meanwhile, the rest of us — a family for whom the promise of death was practically a trade — couldn't bear to acknowledge the fact of his diagnosis.

'Susan Birch.'

It was getting harder to write. This lady — an elderly shopkeeper — I had expected. But Charlie Petter? He had been in my year at school: floppy brown hair pulled over his eyes, a shuffling walk despite his lanky frame due to a rugby injury he sustained in year seven. I saw him...yes, I saw him not just in my mind's eye but a few hundred feet in front of me, as my mother described. A grey figure, grey all over, features almost indistinct. I wanted to call his name to see if he could hear me, but I knew this would be a grave mistake. Susan Birch was just behind, making her way towards the church, the fume of lavender following her. The scent was so familiar it made my head spin.

'George Cooper.'

I wrote this name hastily, desperate to return my gaze to the graveyard procession of the soon-to-be-dead. My pen stuttered, so I span it in my hands to warm up the last few drops of ink. We must almost be through to the other side, I thought, and no mention of Charlie yet. My watch had stopped; I had no measure of time, but it seemed like the frost was beginning to recede. I glanced at my mother, whose warm smile I expected to greet me like the relief of coming home.

You did so well, I willed her to say. I'm proud of you, Maria.

She was not looking at me.

Charlie is going to live another year, I imagined us saying together.

How different his evening must have been compared to mine: white lights, white sheets, the smell of a room doused in antiseptic. A cup of weak tea and a bar of Dairy Milk from a vending machine if Auntie Kim had visited, or a sterile cup of water if not.

Mum was staring at the final figure in the graveyard. Her eyes were not relieved. They were terrified.

Maria Blackwood, I imagined her saying. I felt my own fate unravelling.

But it wasn't my spirit standing in the graveyard.

It was hers.

Chicken Living

When
    I was little, my mum took me to see the chickens.
        They lived in the back garden, scrubbing the ground clean
            of small things. Bossy, pointy, ruffled, they busied
                to and fro, jabbing their little eyes earthward to scour
                    the grass around my feet. I lingered in their meddling
                        clucks, their grabbing heads, scaly claws,
                            stoney unhappy
                              beaks.

I loved
    the chickens so much. So I went back there the next
        day without my mum knowing. I watched their big
            cushion bodies pull and hook on dinosaur legs.
                Running around like I did, minding everyone
                    else's business. So I asked the hens, please can I
                    come and live with you, and they said, sorry,
                      we don't have any
                      vacancies.

I kept
    going back to the chickens to ask them the same
        thing. I chased them around. I giggled at their silly
            prehistoric legs. And their fat feathers. I felt like a
                naughty moppet, because I was one, but I wanted to be a
                chicken. And after a lot of pestering, and running after
                them around prickly bushes, one chicken looked
                at me with her dwarf star eyes and said,
                oh go on then.

So I went
    to live with the chickens. They welcomed me with
        twitching motherly combs into their old wooden houses.
            Feathers flecked with old shavings and dust, warm and
                smelly and poking and frantic. Old jungle claws scratched
                    me to check I was real; delicious white
                  brown liquid smattered on my skin.
                I perched on broken gate posts, nibbled
              on dry brown corn, feeling the
            delicious scratchy earth
        down my neck.

My mum
    found out what I was getting up to and she said,
        you're not a chicken! But what did she know?
            Me and the others raised our little hard red heads
                and ran ran away, kicking up feathered soil, ransacking
                    worms and insects and small grass. And my mother turned to
                despair and thought, what are we going to do?
                        She thinks she's
                        a chicken.

So she hatched
    a plan to get me to leave the chickens.
        We deduced the nature of the plan quite quickly.
            She strode into our home, monstrously wellied.
                Slowly, carelessly, round, and soft, she came for me.
                    We ran madly around but soon she caught me under my
                        feathers. The others clucked clucked angrily. But
                          they were much too small to do anything about
                          it, so I was taken away. And I was taken
                          from my scratchy warmth to
                          sterilised sofas,
                          and I lived like a
                          child should
                          live, which is,
                          not like
                          a chicken.

It's About Time You Got Some Friend's Anyway

It was too busy. Arms and legs streamed out of every doorway. Too busy. Who were these people anyway? Sticky floors and upturned cans suffocated me and was that somebody trying to wee up the wall? My eardrums bubbled and voices melted in cigarette ash.

Why my housemates had decided to have a fucking massive party baffled me.

'As long as they don't go in my room.'
'Well you should lock it then.'
'They better not go in there.'
'Jesus, they won't!' They looked at each other with exasperation and embarrassment.

I got up to leave. Bodies parted with brutish glances and awkward smiles; I bowled myself outside onto the cold black pavement. I looked around me. A large street, familiar but not home.

I was sitting alone, stella in hand, on the sofa. Awkward bodies shuffled in front of me under baggy jeans and mini-skirts and jesus was that someone wearing leggings? After every sip I lost more control of my mouth and cheeks which began to feel loose and numb.

The orange glow of the Sainsbury's fought the supernova of the petrol station nearby and a terrifying grey-haired scowl peered out from behind a papery curtain opposite. Not happy. Anger rose inside me — its only twelve, you've probably got fuck all to do tomorrow anyway.

A family of four lived on our right (poor souls) and funeral home lay on the left. There was always a light on in the home. I wondered who stayed the night, surrounded by those coffins and perfumes and chemicals? What's in there? What if *I* was in there?

—

It must've been the alcohol and the passive rage and to be honest, it felt quite funny, but now I'm halfway through the window and my knee is cut.

The music is still audible here; it beats through the room as a faint pulse. I climb over a metal table sporting leftover lunch and listen closely at a door. I hear movements on the other side and think well I'm here now, so I open it.

Coffins had been moved to the sides of the room like chairs at a school disco. In the middle of the room are four or five figures dancing in the gloom. They are struggling against the music, jerking their limbs around awkwardly. Bodies, pallid, chill, and drear, dressed in crisp suits and old nightgowns, floating in the air and thudding on the fragranced carpet. Their faces are stretched and cold, their skin stretches and sags at irregular intervals.

 I stand still. It seeks my stillness draws them in; they stop their dancing at different times, an unpractised orchestra, and look at me intently, leaning forwards in the soft light with eyes peering inanimately.

 'Are you from the party?' one says, confused.

 'Yes'

 'What are you doing here?' says another.

 'I don't know, I just thought it would be funny really,' I say. 'I don't know.'

 'Oh.'

 It really smells in here. I'm sure I showered this morning. Although I am quite sweaty.

 'Well it's great music,' says one, encouragingly.

 'Thanks. Well, it's not mine really. My housemates chose it.'

 'Oh.'

 A pause.

 'Actually, do you fancy joining us?'

 They look briefly confused but soon break out into wide smiles.

 'We'd love to! Let me just grab my coat.'

—

I wondered if I was making a mistake, whether people might find it a bit weird, but I got over it.

 I led them like ducklings over the table and through the window. 'Careful of the glass'. They stood luminescent in the shadows.

 I stepped inside and led my procession through the hallway into the living room. I sought out a housemate.

 'Is it alright if these guys join?'

 'Who are they?'

 'They're from next door. From the funeral home.'

 He leaned past me and gave them a quick sweep over with judgemental eyes. His mouth curled into a mean smile and his eyelids opened wider as he took their confused-looking forms in.

 'Bit weird isn't it mate?'

'Nah, they're alright.'
He gave them another look and smirked at me.
'Well ok then. It's about time you got some friends, anyway.'

I gave an encouraging smile to the bodies, and they smiled back through the smoky half-light, pale under the disco ball. Soon enough they picked up the same dance I had seen earlier, rocking their limbs unnaturally against the beat. They soon became part of the beer-soaked chairs, the rushed conversations.

People seemed attracted to them somehow, captivated by their movements. Someone asked one of them where the toilet was, and they shrugged apologetically.

I left them to it and drank something and drank some more until my mouth melted away and I couldn't feel the liquid pass through.

Figures swam through the room, and I thought I saw my housemates chatting to the cadavers in the corner, but I thought nothing of it and drank some more. The walls and the chairs cluttered about me, and I felt sick but I held it in and closed my eyes to get my balance but I struggled and spluttered and couldn't open them again.

—

I woke in darkness. I tried to lift my head, but it hit something solid. The air was wood and velvet. I felt for my phone and the bright light stung my eyes. One text.

Sorry mate we kept one of your mates from the party he's in your room, so we put you up at his place, hope that's ok x

I blinked and sighed and rubbed my eyes and went back to sleep.

The Media These Days

'Our Penny's in paper, duck!'
   'Is she really?'
   'That's her, int it?'
   'Looks like her. She's having a good time there isn't she?'
   'Listen to this, I'll read it.'
   'Let me lie down first.'
   'Curl up, love.' '
   Right, I'm ready.'
   'You ready?'
   'I've just told you I'm ready.'
   'Just checking.'
   He snorted and growled the headline out:

<u>FOOTAGE OF PANTHER-LIKE BIG CAT ON DERBYSHIRE FARM</u>

   They looked at each other, eyes wide.

Two teenagers believe they spotted a big cat devouring a dead sheep while walking in the Peak District - and they caught the moment on camera. They say the 'beast' looked like a panther and that they were left shaken by what they had seen.

'Ay, she won't like that, being called a beast. I know she's had her teeth done recently but that's a bit far, she —'
   'Let me read it, Prissy.'
   He scratched and twitched and carried on.

Joshua Williams and his friend were making their way from Mermaid's Pool on Kinder Scout towards Edale, in Derbyshire, on September 26, when they made the sighting. The pair captured the footage following a night of wild camping in the countryside.
   Astounded, Joshua got his phone out and started to film. The 17-year-old told StokeonTrentLive: "I was wild camping with a friend in the Peak District and we believe we spotted a wild cat feeding in a field of sheep as we were walking back to Edale station from our camp spot near Mermaid's Pool.
   I managed to capture a video. It is quite hard to tell what animal this may be but we were so shocked."

'Mermaid's pool? What's she doing up there? Doesn't that no good fella, whatshisname, Pazza, live there? She best not be seeing him, on my life —'
'Calm down you'll wake up every house in ten mile!'
He yawned and licked his lips and kept reading.

But, when the footage was posted on social media, some viewers didn't think it showed a big cat at all, amid suggestions they had merely filmed a bin bag fluttering in the breeze. One woman said: "A person films three seconds of a black bin bag moving slightly in the wind, convinces themselves Bagheera from The Jungle Book has moved to the Peak District."

Another added: "If that was a big cat that sheep would not be chilling so close by. It's probably plastic off a silage bale."

And a further sceptic said: "Amazing all these reports of 'big cats' in the Peak District but never any reports of finding half eaten sheep. Perhaps they are vegetarians."

'Read that again.'
He read it again.
They both lay there, unable to speak. Her bright eyes glimmered in hurt and rage. He felt tense, his heart in a vice.
'They don't think our Penny exists?'
'I don't think they think we exist, duck.'
'How can we not exist? Don't we exist?'
'Of course we do.'
'And our Penny exists, too?'
'Yes, duck.'
'Well why do they think we don't?'
'We're not exactly going to the parish council meetings are we, Prissy.'
'Because, Pete, because they wouldn't listen to us even if we did go! There's no one there interested in supporting our issues!'
He looked at her slowly. Her face was desolate.
'Still. Good for Penny for getting in.'
But she did not reply. She lay her head on her feet and slept for a while.

—

'We've got a feature!'
'Well bring it here then.'

'You're ripping it!'
'Well it's quite difficult, Prissy.'
'Come here.'
'Right.'
The right page fell open. He read.

ARE THERE REALLY BIG CATS IN THE PEAK DISTRICT?

Reported sightings of big cats are a fairly common occurrence in Britain, but the reality behind them is rather more difficult to ascertain. The existence, or otherwise, of a self-sustaining population of big cats in the UK remains a hotly-disputed matter.

However, over the years, the Peak District has been something of a hotspot for alleged sightings of big cats. Last month, two teenagers who were out walking reported seeing a big cat — resembling a panther — devouring a dead sheep, capturing footage which they claimed proved it.

Joshua Williams and a friend were walking from Kinder Scout towards Edale on September 26 when they thought they saw the big cat feeding. But others were sceptical, one commenting that it looked more like "a black bin bag moving slightly in the wind".

'I don't want to hear that old bag again!'
He continued.

Nevertheless, there are many local residents and visitors to the area who have reported seeing animals that look to be much bigger than regular household pets. Since 2007, such sightings have been reported across various parts of the Peak District including the Derbyshire Dales, Amber Valley and Swadlincote, and even in some urban areas.

The only big cat species known to be living wild in the UK is the European Wildcat, which is found in the Scottish Highlands. However, there are some big cat aficionados adamant that there are others prowling the British countryside — including the Peak District.

It's not completely beyond the realms of possibility that there are some big cats in the Peak District. It has been suggested that some exotic pets, held illegally, may have escaped, or been released when they proved to be too challenging to keep.

Danny Bamping, of the British Big Cat Society, told WalesOnline that any big cats living in the wild would be "a mixture of hybrids and ferals". These hybrids may be the offspring of larger cats, he explained, though any such animals would be unable to breed themselves.

"You can also have hybrids from larger cats that have interbred. So there is the opportunity of finding something unique in the British Isles in terms of a feline that is a hybrid," he said. "When they become hybridised, that's where the DNA stops because they can't breed."

But concrete evidence to prove that there are big cats living in the British countryside still seems to be largely lacking. This is unlikely, however, to stop the purported sightings from rolling in - even if they are just bin bags flapping in the wind.

Once again, they turned to look at each other, speechless, utter unhappiness written on their faces.

'Exotic pets?'
'Terrible, duck.'
'Hybrids and ferals?'
'I know.'
'Right.'
'What?'
'Right.'
'What, Prissy?'
'I'm going down there.'
'Down where?'
'To the newspaper.'
'They won't listen.'
'They bloody well will listen.'
'They won't —'

But before he could growl out his sentence, she stalked out, pawing the ground angrily, and with purpose.

—

'How did it go?'
'Pack the bags.'
'What bags? What happened?'
'I can't stay here anymore.'
'Why not?'

'They're *ignorant*, Pete.'

'What happened?'

'Well. I walked up, and well, after some initial terror, which I have to say was a bit over the top and involved a lot of flapping, they agreed to see me. Well, that was a false promise, they kept me waiting for two hours, two hours Pete, and when I got in there I gave the editor a piece of my mind. I told her, you journalists, you have a duty, an obligation, for fair representation. I told her that labelling our Penny, and all of us for that matter, a "beast" and an "exotic pet" and "hybrids and ferals" was deeply troubling, deeply offensive. But then, I told her, she doesn't stop there, she actually denies our very existence and pretends we don't breathe the same air and read the same shit in the papers. Well, I told her, that takes some nerve. I told her that it's a dangerous game, publishing things like that, and the media these days is going to the dogs, and if she's not careful she'll end up right at the bottom of the quagmire with the lot of them!'

She panted heavily.

'And what then?'

'I left, and she sat there gormless. Not surprised really.'

'I see.'

'That's right.'

'Well.'

They sat. The air was poised.

'Well, let's get ready to go then.'

'To go?'

'Pack the bags.'

'Where we going?'

'I've always fancied France.'

One Last Breath

At the age of fifty-seven and three-quarters, Josephine Stuart decided that it was time to die. It wasn't that she was particularly sad about anything. She was just quite tired now. Besides, according to the latest prophecy by a climate-change activist she religiously followed on YouTube, the world was going to come to an end by the time she reached sixty anyway.

    She wasted no time planning her death. Josephine dictated her funeral plan to her hamster, Harry, who had learnt to type long ago. He did like to improvise sometimes, so she always had to double-check what the rat, who was quite prone to vulgarity, had written down. "I will be wrapped in sheepskin, and buried in my Gucci flats," Josephine recited. *I will be wrapped in clingfilm and buried in only my hat*, typed Harry with a squeak. Peering down at the screen, Josephine swatted his head causing him to fly across the table, knocking over a glass of wine in the bargain, which spilt all over the carefully drawn coffin layouts. Josephine decided that the best way to tackle the mess would be to leave the house and deal with it later. She dumped her phone, a little digital camera, and a half-eaten sandwich into a bag, and set off in the direction of the bridge-to-the-Cathedral.

    There was a sharp chill in the air, and she wrapped her scarf tight around her neck. For the past decade she had walked along that bridge every day. She knew every stone on the cobbled footpath, she had memorised exactly how many steps it took to reach the wooden archway, and she knew where to stand to get the best view of the village. She walked to that spot and fished out her camera, balancing it precariously on the edge of the railing, just like she had done five hundred and seventy-five times before, as per her latest Google Photos update. With a practised flick of the wrist, she pressed the button down. But just as the little click went off, a seagull swooped down and grabbed the gadget in its claws. Josephine shrieked. And then she lunged. Josephine couldn't tell precisely what possessed her to react the way she did. Before she knew it, she had leapt into the sky after the bird. Maybe Josephine had underestimated her own ability to high jump; Maybe it was particularly windy that day; Maybe it was fate. The wind seemed to catch her body like a rope, yanking her over the railing until gravity took over and pulled Josephine head-first into the water. She catapulted into the river, legs flailing, the hem of her skirt now at her ears. Right before her head hit the water in an almost perfect dive, she hoped she was wearing her good underwear.

    Her body hit the icy water and it sucked her in instantly. She said a silent prayer, grateful for the ten years of Commando training that had equipped her to stay comfortably underwater for four and a half minutes.

As she sunk deeper into the river, the weight of her heavy skirt and scarf pulled her down like a cockroach might be sucked into the deathly abyss of a vacuum cleaner. Suddenly, she became aware of an audience. Floating around her were four creatures. The centaur-like beings had the face of a human, the body of a horse and the tail of a fish. A set of wing-like fins protruded from their bellies on either side and flapped elegantly in the water. Sea-centaurs! She had a sneaking suspicion that they were the culprits behind all the floods that year. Every time a sea centaur flew into a rage, the river would overflow its banks, Josephine's grandmother used to tell her.

She opened her mouth to tell them off about the terrible condition the floods had left her garden in, but then she remembered she was holding her breath. A soft voice began to speak. The voice seemed to float towards her, barely audible, but if she believed in angels, Josephine was sure this is what they would sound like. "We've been waiting for one of you," a sea-centaur with long golden hair said in an eerie echo. "Come," the creature ordered. One of the larger of the sea-centaurs glided through the water and came to rest in front of Josephine. "Hop on," he said in an angelic whisper. Josephine, rather excited at the prospect of an underwater ride, grabbed onto its flowing hair. She had almost forgotten she needed to breathe.

What happened next was one of the more peculiar things to have happened in Josephine's life. (And she was a woman who had climbed Mount Kilimanjaro barefoot, married (and divorced) a Spanish matador and single-handedly rescued 17 puppies from Loreal's illegal and never-exposed testing centre.) In a gentle canter-like glide, the sea-centaur glided through the murky water with Josephine clinging on tight. The rest of the creatures followed close behind, keeping in a strict triangular formation. In less than twenty seconds, they had arrived at a magnificent shipwreck. Little silver eels slithered on the algae-covered deck that shone with a fierce bioluminescent glow. Streaks of light emanated from what must have once been the captain's cabin. Through narrowed eyes burning with the sting of the lake water, Josephine thought that if this was the last thing she ever saw, she was glad it was a sunken ship that still shone.

The sea-centaur glided down some stairs that led to the remains of a banquet hall where there seemed to be a gathering of lake creatures. On the stage, there stood a massive sea- centaur with golden wings outstretched and a beard that swayed with the current, wrapping itself around its owner's neck like a serpent. Lines of pearl mussels and mud snails assembled in groups making a rather oddly-themed cocktail party. A deep voice that sounded like the tenor in a choir spoke out loud, addressing Josephine:

"Oh land creature, from up high
You venture close by
Has fate called you in,
To live your last sin?"

Confusion must have registered on Josephine's face because the sea-centaur began to laugh. A terrifying sound that filled up the entire room. Dropping his poetic form, he continued. "Just kidding, little one. We have been waiting for a human to drop down from the sky. It so happens that my son has reached the marriageable age of 537 years, and I wish for him to partner with a pure human." In spite of her current near-drowning state, Josephine felt herself blush at the prospect of a romantic entanglement with an exotic stranger. Especially at her age, it was most unexpected. "It's all part of our Human-Sea-Centaur Mating for Peace Programme," he explained in his sing-song voice. "For years, we have been blamed for the unprecedented floods that destroy human houses. But it is not us who is responsible. It is the humans. Your species has destroyed up to 70% of the Earth's natural ponds, rivers, and seas. And if they don't stop now - our home will disappear. We will all be doomed."

Josephine had just about a minute left of air in her large and well-cared-for lungs. But she was now terrified not just for her own life, but for that of the entire world. This year's floods could destroy a lot more than just her strawberries. "Josephine, if you match with my son — then perhaps we can begin to bridge both our worlds together so that we may make the planet safe again. Are you with us?"

Josephine was filled with a great sense of purpose. She had a mission. She had to save the world. She tried to open her mouth to accept the proposal, but instead water filled her chest, burning her insides like she was on fire. Her eyes felt like they were exploding out of their sockets as her body twisted and turned in a grotesque dance of death. The sea-centaurs and snails and mussels began to crowd around her, getting closer and closer. She looked up and saw a sliver of light beaming down at her like a wisp of grey hair floating in the dark. For the first time in a long time, Josephine didn't want to die.

10 YEARS LATER:
They never found Josephine's body. But the floods never harmed the village again, and the Earth still spins stronger and greener than ever before.

Flame of the Forest

By the beginning of March, the forest transforms from wintery grey and pastel green to the colour of rust and honey. The birds rise a little earlier, the animals venture out a little longer. The humans continue like nothing much had really happened.

    The mixed deciduous forests of Satpura can be deceptive for a newcomer. Every few kilometres the landscape changes vividly. Lush green plains give way to forests of teak and sal. Riverine gorges empty into dry, sandy plains, spreading their sticky fingers between the rocks that provide perfect camouflage for the sandgrouse waddling on the forest floor. The foothills of Satpura are bathed with an orange glow as the mahua trees begin to flower, shedding their bright shell to form a crisp carpet below. The sweet scent of the petals fill the forest, inviting a host of visitors to its hallowed boughs. Monkeys swing from branches, reaching for the sweetest buds with ease, greedy fingers plucking them eagerly, stuffing their faces while red juice drips down their furry jaws. The heavy branches of the mahua bow down like loyal subjects in the court of the sun. Humans from the village nearby arrive with big baskets to collect the flowers fallen on the ground. Ten kilograms of mahua can make enough to feed a family for a week. The petals are crushed and fermented to form a strong liquor that is sold in the market. Whatever doesn't sell is kept at home to drown away the sorrows that befall the people who venture too close to the wild.

She waited for sunrise to leave the hut. The mud floor was cool underneath her feet as she tied her hair in a braid and caught a glimpse of herself in the little mirror on the wall. She picked up a long, sturdy stick with one hand and hoisted a straw basket on her hip with the other. Her brother lay fast asleep on the mattress behind her, undisturbed by her morning routine.

    She had made this journey a hundred times before, but the first collection of spring was always special. She wanted to be the first one at the tree. The first one to pick a red flower off the floor and watch it fall to the bottom of her basket. The first of many petals, the first of the fortune of spring. She skipped along the trail, her slippers slapping against the cement track built by the new safari lodge that had appeared that winter. Sunbirds and warblers chattered around her and a kingfisher, blue-green wings outstretched, sat perched on the power lines that ran along the side of the road. A jeep roared by, interrupting the silence of the morning. She waved gleefully at the three ladies in the back wearing hats and sunglasses, binoculars and cameras hanging around their necks. They waved back at her, holding on to their hats as the jeep whizzed by, pointing their cameras at her face. She kept waving, growing smaller and smaller on their screens, until she disappeared from their view. The morning was hers once again.

The tree was marked with a yellow cloth. Her brother had tied it there the previous afternoon, a clear warning to the other villagers that no one else could pluck mahua from it. She lay the straw basket on the ground and surveyed the land before her. Flowers, dark pink and red lay delicately strewn across the floor like a rangoli pattern that someone had accidentally walked over. She squatted down and began to pick the petals one by one, admiring the beauty of their shape and feel. The underside of the petal was velvet to touch, and she placed it tenderly against her cheek. Her mother would be so happy that she had come early to pick the flowers before they were wilted from the morning sun. She couldn't wait to show off her collection. She tucked a petal behind her ear and giggled, imagining that she was a young Madhuri Dixit twirling and dancing among the trees.

She lost track of time as the level of petals in her basket gradually inched higher, until she became aware of a sudden silence. The usual chatter of the birds had died down. The earth seemed to be listening for something. She listened too. A piercing call suddenly ripped through the air, followed by the sound of panic-stricken hoofbeats falling on hard mud. A langur shrieked nearby. Too close for comfort.

Her heart grew cold. A predator was on the prowl and the creatures of the forest were doing their best to warn each other of its presence.

She heard it before she saw it. Heavy steps treading on dry leaves. Her heart hammered into her chest loudly as though it was trying to complete a lifetime of work in a few precious seconds. She clenched her fists, still holding onto the red petals that were now crushed and embedded into her sweaty palms. Her body was rigid with fear. Her stick lay forgotten on the ground next to her, little use against what was approaching. She had heard stories before. She had sat around a fire at night and listened intently to tales of her ancestor's battles with the cats of the forest. Her great uncle, the legendary tiger slayer, had killed a beast with his bare hands. Perhaps this was revenge.

The tiger emerged from the thick undergrowth calmly, as though unaware that its presence had caused the entire forest to stop breathing. The young girl crouched beside the mahua tree as though seeking assurance from its strong trunk. The cat stopped to look at her. A large male with muscles that ripped across his chest and legs, he glowered at her, surveying the pitiful sight with the eyes of a practised killer.

Their eyes met, predator and prey. It was impossible for either to look away.

Donkey Breath

Miguel is sat upright with perfect posture in a dental practice waiting room. His face is stern and long; his nose droops owing to missing cartilage; his cheeks are rosy and cherubic-chubby and beneath small eyebags; his jaw is long and sharp and in a downwards trajectory; his eyes are good and brown, and his charcoal hair has buzzed away to spotlight a sound hairline.

He is sat alone. He does not like the radio show playing smooth jazz because it is making him drowsy, and he would like to be awake when the receptionist enters the room calling his card. The walls of this waiting room are lined with wooden frame chairs that have a blue fabric cushioned seat. Miguel recalls his days of his internship where such chairs were plenty. He finds them boring and basically offensive to a workplace that "inspired creativity", even for an accountant such as he.

The day is Monday. It is one of his "health days": a self-administered day of the month where he books all necessary health-related appointments into one day. He starts off today with this dentist appointment, later he will attend a general GP check-up, then a physio for a sore hip/bum, then lunch, then the opticians and concluding with a therapy session. Such a list of appointments each month are never necessary for someone as basically bodily fine as Miguel, but it is something for him to do. You see, his work is only a part-time, work-at-home job and he feels lazy if he does nothing on every day off, therefore: health days. He even dresses in work attire. He does not wear such attire while working at home.

Miguel gets funny feelings about waiting rooms. It is a fairly common phenomenon often mistaken for uncanniness. Miguel finds that the idea of the uncanny does not do his feelings credit. Waiting rooms, as well as pylons, LED headlights and laptop keyboards that require little if any pressure to command their function, give Miguel a very real physical reaction. Not like anything nauseating or headache begetting, but more of a pleasant lightness in his head or an unpleasant psychosomatic push on his cheeks. For Miguel, the phenomenon is an indescribable sensation. But this annoys him, too, because he believes the word "indescribable" cannot exist: if something is "indescribable", it is not. This is because "indescribable" itself is an adjective and therefore being utilised as a means of description. As the word is spoken, it collapses in on itself. "Indescribable" is a self-made contradiction. The word exists, and therefore, it should not exist.

This particular waiting room does not really smell of anything, nor does it urge a contentment to "wait". For Miguel, it is more like an "anticipation room", the receptionist ushers you inside and as a consequence you cannot wait to get out. His two appointments that have such waiting rooms (the dentist and GP) are scheduled first, to get the worst out of the way.

The waiting room door opens. 'If you'd like to follow me, please,' the receptionist says to Miguel. He does as he is offered and follows the receptionist down the short hall. The carpet is a similar blue to the chair cushions, but pricklier looking. The receptionist stops at the end of the hallway and gestures his room to enter. She smiles as she leaves him.

Miguel enters and completes the standard procedure with the same dentist and dentist's assistant he has met monthly for the past three or so years. It is not long before his blazer is strewn over a spare chair near the door, and he is laying supine on the navy orthodontic chair. The dentist rolls over from the computer on her rollychair and reclines Miguel with a foot pedal.

While the dentist and the dentist's assistant do their dental rounds, Miguel thinks entirely of nothing. Exactly zero thoughts race through his brain. He does not think of the day ahead; he does not think of his friends; he does not think of work; he does not think of his ex-girlfriend; he does not think of the future; he only experiences the experience of being a customer at this specific dental practice. He feels the sickle probe scrape, the suction device collect his saliva, he sees the mouth mirror go in his mouth and then come out.

Miguel is then handed some safety goggles and a bib. The assistant hands a paper cup of mouth rinse for him to gurgle and spit down a pipe of sorts. He gets up and out of the chair and sticks and unsticks his tongue as he builds his saliva back. He puts on his blazer, says and waves goodbye to the dentist, dentist's assistant and then the receptionist as he takes his leave of the place. He unlocks and enters his car. There is no noise anywhere. He begins to cry a bit but shakes it off as he strikes the ignition and drives over to his GP.

The GP is located only a ten-minute drive from the dental practice and so he enjoys the drive casually, no need to rush. His playlist soundtracks the journey smoothly: a bit of Leonard Cohen, a bit of Current 93. It is still morning, so the kids are at school and the adults are talking at work. He drives on.

He pulls into the scarce carpark, locks up and heads on in. He registers his presence at reception and walks into the waiting room, taking a seat on the same, blue-cushioned chair model of the dental practice. There is one older man keeping him company, though Miguel has sat himself across the room from him. No harm done; the man is asleep.

 Miguel once more sits in a waiting room with perfect posture. This posturing is yet to be an unconscious act (as he soon hopes it will). He started his posture habits only around two months ago, when he noted his bulbous gut which he credited to beer. Since then, he has ordered only spirits with mixers from pubs and tried to develop postural improvements. He will become annoyed with himself while he sits at his work desk at home and grows suspicious of his bodily comfort. Miguel is finding it difficult to maintain these habits; he is aware of the long-term benefits, yet he knows full well he won't be able to slouch when he reaches such and such an age and is therefore stuck between making the most of his youthful durability, or postponing back pain and a crooked neck. Miguel once read an online article relating to postural habit, a few lines of which read: *Slouching too often can lead to gastrointestinal complications, it can also lead to poor mental health. The shape of the spine affects the shape of the spinal cord; the spinal cord is important in matters of the mind. The whole body is connected, and a large section of the body is the torso, this truncal structure is nearly exclusively dependant on the spine.*

 The waiting room door opens. 'If you'd like to follow me, please,' the receptionist says to Miguel. He does as he is offered and follows the receptionist down a short hall, going past reception. He is shown into a room halfway down the hall on his left-hand side and his familiar doctor, following introductions, continues where they both left off a month ago.

 Miguel sits in a chair similar to those in the waiting room, against the wall and directly adjacent to the doctor's desk. His eyeline is perfect for contact with both the doctor and the barricaded window to the doctor's left which looks out over the car park and onto the church just next door.

 The doctor asks Miguel routine questions, and Miguel replies with routine answers. It seems there is no complaints from either people in the room. Miguel sits comfortably and, once again, little to nothing enters his mind. He feels comfortably numbed by his doctor and the room he is sat in. The room is fit only for the adjective: "standard". The floor is of the same material as that of the dentist's office floor: sheet vinyl with some weird glitter about it. It was a bit sticky under Miguel's brogues.

 He soon leaves the doctors and heads off to his physiotherapist. The playlist resumes again, this time sounding out some Swans and Roy Orbison.

Miguel is now laying prone on the treatment table while his familiar physiotherapist rubs some nebulous gel on his right glute and upper hamstring. The physiotherapist rubs deep, and Miguel can feel their fingers like he can feel his tongue against his teeth, as if a part of him. This time he is attentive, this is because he enjoys chatting with the physiotherapist. The physiotherapist, without fail, always asks Miguel to remind them where he is from, and so, when he replies, 'just a few miles south of here', the physio, as per, replies with, 'ah yes, of course! What am I like?'

The physiotherapist wipes the gel off his leg with some paper towels before washing their hands and tells Miguel to turn onto his back. He does as such and enacts the various stretches the physio advises, he feels a slight tinge in his lower bum, but nothing to concern himself with. Miguel notes how these stretches can become a part of his daily routine which should spark his postural corrections.

Miguel is in his car now and off to get lunch. While laying prone during the silent minutes on the treatment table he had one thought, and that concerned his hunger. He decided on some sushi. He drives to a big shop, buys some sushi, and eats it in his car with a window down. He finishes eating, exits his car, puts the rubbish in a bin and returns to his car. He takes a sip of a drink and checks his watch; his opticians booking is in twenty minutes time. The drive to the opticians from this car park is roughly fifteen minutes. He drives off, resuming his playlist: some more Roy Orbison, a 22-20s track and a song by Zappa.

He now sits in the opticians. There is no waiting room as such for the opticians, there is only two sections to the practice. On entering off the high street, you walk past the presentation of various glasses and sunglasses, you walk up to a lady behind a desk and tell them the intentions of your visit. She will then confirm your appointment and point her finger over her shoulder as she informs you to take a seat around the other side of that wall over there. The wall juts out toward the backend of the opticians and is invisible to the shopfront. From any seat in this waiting section, you will only be able to see a water cooler, a poster or two advertising eyewear brands, and the other people around you.

Miguel is sat by himself, routine posture. The carpet is maroon and prickly like that of the hallway of the dental practice. The chairs are the same as those of the GP and the dentists, too, but with a maroon cushion. Miguel rubs both his hands up and down the armrest of the chair, feeling the acrylic wood. Once again, he recalls his internship office.

Miguel is now inside the office of the familiar optometrist. Following introductory protocol, he rests his chin in a tonometer. Next, Miguel has one of his eyes under cover of darkness and the other is interpreting a shuffled-up mirror-reversed alphabet. He then does the same with his other eye.

The optometrist is now partly reclining in their desk chair and is asking Miguel about any possible causes for complaint ('any excessive headaches?'; 'No strain while reading or watching tele?'). While this questioning continues, Miguel, thanks to a swivel in the optometrist chair and thereby a different lighting casting down, notices abundant wrinkling about the face of this eye doctor. Miguel begins to wonder whether the optometrist had always looked like this and whether the ballpark estimate he has of their age is amiss by something near a decade? Pairing the lucid face-wear with the poor postural recline, Miguel got curious: 'What is the age of this optometrist?'; 'Do the wrinkles come with said age?'; 'Is he not in pain?'; 'He looks near on seventy'; 'Has he sat like this his whole life?'; 'I assumed he was something like fifty before'; 'Sit up straight man'; 'His dying days will be spent two feet shorter'; 'Or, maybe, has this optometrist practiced sound posture all his life and is only now making most of his bodily capabilities?'

Miguel likes his optometrist very much. He found himself smiling during their questioning. It was much more like a conversation. Soon enough, though, the optometrist was showing Miguel the door. No need for glasses.

Miguel now walks back up the high street, enjoying the cold air diluted by the sun. He walks up and past of his bus-stops he stood at during his school days and recalls it was where he smoked his first cigarette. Further up the road, he enters an off-license and buys a pack of twenty cigarettes, he then walks back down the street, and recreates the scene to the best of his ability. He did not do as such out of some longing to realise to live retroactively, no, he just did it because he felt like it, and because he knew he had about ten minutes to kill before he needed to head off for his therapy session.

In the car now, and Miguel is driving out of town and therapy bound. The playlist resumes with some Beatles, Alanis Morissette, and Burial. He forces any memories of his last therapy session out of mind, knowing he will recall all just fine when the familiar door opens, and his familiar seat is occupied.

Miguel pulls his car outside the house of his therapist. At first sceptical of the professional merit of therapy being conducted in a house inside the heart of an affluent suburb, Miguel has since come round to appreciate where he is currently parked. With a few minutes to kill still, he sits in his car and thinks of the business parks or big office buildings he could have unfortunately been assigned to.

It is early afternoon, and it seems Dr. Haag has no current patient, Miguel therefore knocks on her home a few minutes early. Dr Haag welcomes him inside. Upon entering, Miguel is met with a smell that is nearly identical to the smell of every suburban home, something generally antiseptic seems fit. His ears prickle as he closes the door behind him, and he walks on through and down the hallway, hearing his brogues tip-tap past the stairs, ground floor toilet and bowl of potpourri freshening up the coatrack vicinal before entering the session-room at the far-right end of the ground floor.

Dr. Haag has a cup of tea waiting for Miguel on a coffee table next to his familiar chair, the steam is salient as the sun comes on through the bay windows. Dr. Haag also had a cup of tea set up on a different coffee table next to her familiar chair, less light reached that side of the room. Dr. Haag is wearing loose-fit jeans and a matching, blue-washed hoodie, with some very furry slippers too. Her posture is very good, Miguel notices.

Miguel was wrong to at first assume that this was all an act, that Dr. Haag hosting sessions in her own home and wearing what is not even smart-casual and putting herself and the client in chairs so plump that a cushion would make the chair a beanbag of cow shit and letting the client close the door behind themselves and saying 'Hey' and not 'Welcome' or, say, 'You must be _____', but 'Hey' on very first introductions — this whole rigmarole, Miguel was wrong to assume, was surely a test. Surely that when the session ends and the client has shown themselves out, Dr. Haag would strip off and hurry into a three-piece and run into her real office which is basically just a room with a doughnut desk in the centre and a wall of multiple televisions that function as the big brothers and, with their whatever kind of new technology, circle, highlight, zoom in, slow down, and perfectly display the various cameras and microphones they are connected to. That this rigmarole was an act, that the Dr. Haag you talk with and tell your fears and open up to was not a genuine person, was a harsh prejudice. What Miguel sees, actually, Miguel gets.

Miguel blows the steam off his tea and takes a first sip. Dr. Haag and

Miguel make good time and are getting to the beginning of their session now.

The two begin a discussion. Miguel remembers where they left off and is comfortable to talk with Dr. Haag for the next two hours. He is very relaxed and drifts through the conversation kinda outside of himself. He is surprised by the simplicity and yet profundity with which his turns of talk come out of him.

This stops though, when Dr. Haag brings up the topic which, up until now, Miguel genuinely did not think about, and which Dr. Haag has been leading toward.

'[...], and how often do you think of your friend, Ribs?' asks Dr. Haag.
(beat)
'Somehow I didn't think about you mentioning him today,' says Miguel, with a feeling of his throat sunken to his intestines.
'Don't you want to talk about it? We don't have to.'
'What is there to talk about, y'know?'
'It's a big thing to happen. It happened to you, too.'
'I'm aware, doc.'
'You sure?'
'Yeh I'm sure. I know what death's about. I'm aware that I'm one of the people it happened to. It happened; it can't be unhappened. What do you want me to say?'
'Maybe any feelings you have about the event, that's all.'
'Genuinely, without trying to be all mysterious and cool about this, I just don't have that many strong feelings about it. I'm not in denial either, I know it happened.'
'Ok. And what about what you told me last week?'
'What about it?'
'It seems quite important to me, that's all, Miguel.'
'You've looked into this more than you needed to, doc. I don't see him in any literal way. I'm well aware he's not actually there, or literally speaking to me like you are right now. I don't really see him and hear him, I just imagine he's here sometimes, but it takes quite a bit of my brain power to perform that, y'know?'
'Is he here now?'
'HaHa! Ah, fuck you, man. I've not gone schizo alluva sudden. Is that what you seriously think? Since last week have you honestly, like whenever you've looked and seen my name in your schedule have you gone like, oh

yeh the schizoboy?! Here comes the schizoboy!' Miguel says this in more of an annoyed voice than an angry one.
'You know I don't Miguel, c'mon. I believe you, really, I do. It's not my job to speculate.'
'No, he's not here in the room with me.'
'Ok, thank you.'
'Though I *can* see my father masturbating into the fireplace.'
'Oh, yea?'
'Big time.'
'I'll jot that down,' giggles Dr. Haag. 'Now, Miguel, your friend is gone,' (It is true that Ribs is dead. He killed himself about two months ago. Ribs is dead.) 'and no one can take that away from you.'
'I don't want it to be taken from me. I know his death is mine. His death is many other people's too, but for me it's mine,' Miguel says, before he drinks his cold tea whole. 'make of that what you will.'
'Do you remember when you told me about your friend's passing?'
'No, but I can imagine it was after he died.'
'It was about two months ago, Miguel, and you told me with the face you have now, a seemingly unfazed face. I cannot help if you cannot tell me what's behind the face.'
'So, help me help you help me to tell you how I feel.'
'You'd like to talk about talking about your feelings?'
'Why not?'
'Because you're not talking about Ribs, Miguel.'
'You said it yourself, though, I can't.'
'So, you'd like help in opening up?'
'Can that be arranged?'
'Of course it can. I'll always do the best I can.'
'Good.'
'So, you ok with being here for the long haul, huh?'
'I'd like to live for as long as my mind will have me, I've told you this. Sometimes that will mean giving it some of the things it wants to, I'll let my body look and feel how it pleases, but if I can really understand some things that are base about me I think I'll figure some stuff out easier. It'll help me foresee some stuff.'
'Being here is a good thing for you, Miguel.'
'Of course. Ribs remains dead, though.'
(beat)
'Ribs is dead,' Miguel repeats. 'Ribs is dead.'

Pride Pin Badge

In my first year at university, my friend gave me a Pride Pin badge. A small, metallic circle with weight. Everywhere I went, Pride emblazoned the outward-facing side of my Tote bag; as I went food shopping at the local supermarket, or watched films at the big chain cinema by the Workingmen's pub. It was present whenever I studied at the public library, and on the walks to pre-drinks at friend's houses, cans of Gin and Tonic cluttering up those cobblestoned hills. It travelled before I did, swinging a fraction ahead as I moved, guiding my newly independent routine into fruition.

This routine of work, walk, work, walk inspired a sense of newfound autonomy. My self-worth skyrocketed. I'm sure I was not the only one; self-important people enjoy hearing their own voice. University was fertile for an oversaturation of talk. Conversations were everything to be had. The friends I had made in my first two weeks — one of whom, Amelie, the friend who gifted me the pin — were all extremely chatty and unfamiliar to me. The university town we lived in was a medieval circus of cafes and bars and libraries and bookshops which facilitated their brilliance; my awe-inspired ear. It made having conversations probable at any given time, and this probability doubled when people noticed my Tote bag. 'Nice badge!' and 'You on the committee?', pointing to the pin, were phrases I became used to hearing. This tiny accessory enriched my life with close friends and confidants who I chatted to at length about anything and everything. The late autumn sun spread a gauzy warmth over the city and each day I woke with a renewing amiability pooling inside my chest.

My world quickly folded out into a socio-political chess board. It became important to discuss the 'important people' on the campus. Over steaming cups of coffee I had all manners of conversations ranging from whether the Principle of so-and-so college was secretly homophobic, or if the head of the Student Union was actively disengaging from the LGBT+ club scene out of some hidden agenda. Each conversation was startling and fresh, as if we few rested on top of a precipice peering down upon others. I became woozy on the illusioned power. However, we could never come to an agreement; someone always became disillusioned at someone else, someone's friend was the Working-Class Representative and so discussion was off limits, or occasionally the people we spoke about stepped down and suddenly lost all importance. Sometimes I would spin my pin badge round and round as I spoke to the group, lost within my own words and their onlooking eyes. We all took it very seriously. Even when a male third year cautioned against a college's dining hall on a superstition that masculine presenting women were given smaller portions to 'waste back into femininity,' we all nodded in unison, gripped.

After a couple of months of constant use, the pin would wrestle free and occasionally stab me in the side of my stomach. I realised that after all, a certain pain was to be expected by wearing it. My free-time practically dried out and, being out of my accommodation so often, the flat surfaces in my room — the desk, windowsill, bedside table — all grew a thick layer of dust. The bonsai tree gifted from my mother died overnight. A brittle layer of brown and rustic red by the window lined in silent decay around the pot itself, a small graveyard of my own creation. I remember throwing it into the bin with the post-it note my mother had attached. 'Good luck at university! Water me every time you miss home' felt like a mockery of my situation and only pushed me from maintaining contact. It was not guilt, but an unassailable desire to live in the present. After this episode, my schedule thickened into a concrete wall of coffee, cafés, and conferences in which I conversed effortlessly, mindlessly, about those things I thought so shiny and mature.

I came to realise the badge was a key that had unlocked a certain subculture within the university. One in which friendships and social standing were measured by the amount of new information you gathered and produced day by day, or how attentive and passive you might be in providing an ear for another person's rant. I'm not sure at what point I turned it into a game — maybe it always had been — but I kept playing it because it was an achievement, to finally fit in socially, and I was good at it. To find my people, whether or not they bothered to ask me about my problematic parents or the ladder of scars on my wrist. I felt vindicated somewhat, to know that by simply sitting in silence, offering the occasional quick-witted remark or cutting comment, I could make friends.

When I moved back home for the Christmas holidays, I unpinned the Pride pin from my tote and abandoned it in my upper desk drawer to collect dusk alongside a collection of cress seeds and fairy lights. This was not out of forgetfulness but out of self-preservation: my family had still not come to terms entirely with my sexuality. My mother would still slip up and lump me in with the other people of 'my kind' over casserole dinner, and my dad continued to mutter the f-slur under his breath whilst we all watched a pride march shut down the streets of Manchester on BBC News. My grandad's mantra that 'every good boy should be seen, not heard' was a queasy echo that bounced off the walls of my bedroom. Like a silent movie,

I lived in supressed mute the entire month and rarely left my bed. My life at university had made me aware of my position as the family's black sheep in startling new colours. I dreamt of returning to the cafés that lined the high street and the club nights where men wore makeup that resembled the colours and contours of an entire rainforest; pale blues, vermillion reds and purples, and vibrant pinks and greens, like those of a venus fly trap.

I saw my 'home' friends less frequently and conversations felt forced somehow. Our relations soured like a glass of warm milk that had grown a slimy, congealed layer over the top. There was a discomfort brought on by unfamiliarity. Not one of us knew how to overcome this. One friend returned with a pierced nose. It was a crimson, scabbed thing on the septum that she regularly scratched and poked. Another friend spoke of a boyfriend none of us had ever met. She acted as if he were the only person on the planet that existed and often ditched our group FaceTimes to be with him. Naturally, I told them of my new friends and all the cafes we would go to when they visited. I'm not sure they listened; we were all engrossed in our new lives. All we wanted was a mirror to tell our lives to. To be listened to without interruption, for our new independent lives to mean something to someone. To confirm these signs of life as irrevocably ours to keep. I was certain we all came away from the Christmas break annoyed and confused at who we each had become in that short space of time, and slightly melancholy as time passed us by. Our weekly FaceTimes slowed and, by the end of the second term, had dried up altogether.

The holidays confirmed many things for me at the time; my desire for the rough cocktail of clubbing, hook-ups and coffee dates at university, my hatred for my parents antiquated and obscene views on everything, and life as an inherently self-centred and narcissistic endeavour. The past became something so distant and obscured that I let it have little impact over my life at all. I remember occasionally deleting my mother and father's contacts in my phone just to see if it would change anything. It didn't, but I did it anyway.

After returning from the Christmas holidays, I met my Pride badge with the drive of an animal finding a watering hole in the desert. Primal. Second term was a gut punch that whipped the air from my lungs. I had a thirst to forget everything except the little bubble I surrounded myself in. Those few friends who showed an interest in my mental state, I'd rejected. They cared too much, and I did not like the moments seeing their worry-worn faces as they openly questioned me. They reminded me of my parents.

Instead, I ran towards any sort of impermanence; nights blown open with nitrous oxide, spliffs rolled sleek and slim under shaking fingers, dimly lit Uber interiors yet drivers that I came to recognise by name, face, and number plate. A belt untying, plastic crinkling in a drunken grip, muffles skirting around dark rooms, one penultimate groan, then the guilty stillness of pipes pumping water behind walls. Cold and untouchable. Afterwards, I would float back to my accommodation across town, untethered in a pre-dawn ectoplasm that disguised choked sobbing with airy birdsong.

Then came Spring. The clocks span forward and students waltzed through town with renewed energy as if they were the kin of the weeds and ferns that had magically sprouted from the riverbeds overnight. I did not understand how they managed. During the daytime, I moved between sleep and the library with little comprehension of my surroundings, stuck in a state of repressed consciousness. The Pin badge never left my room for I never went out except for essentials. I fell behind on every one of my essays. I had worn out my tutor's 'benefit of the doubt' with constant grovelling and fake illnesses. I was playing catch up in a game that never seemed to end. It was not surprising that I became increasingly depressed. I could feel it in myself, as a turtle recedes back into their shell.

My friends quickly caught onto my alteration in mood. Instead of extending their help or company, they turned away into the nearest source of gossip, leaving me to work alone. It appears I was a failure in their eyes; not solely because I failed to provide new drama, but because my mood was a hindrance on their events. Slowly, over the course of the second term, they made new group chats and scheduled secret events that I did not know about. I only realised this when I saw a group of people, including Amelie, in a coffee shop we had frequented in first term. I turned from the window with goosebumps dressing my shoulders and called in sick to my mentor meeting. Without people whom I felt I could talk to, I became a complete hermit. When the essay results came back, I wanted to cry. I wanted to call my mother. But when I went to find her contact in my phone, I realised that she was not there. I had deleted her, and my father, a few weeks before.

That was all a couple of weeks ago. Now, my lungs are full-to-bursting with cigarette smoke, my eyelids stained the fuschia-pink of day-old eyeshadow. My lower lip is cracked and trainers muddied; Adidas logo faded to indecipherable shadow. The once delicate embroidery of my shirt is now a patchwork of a stranger's public toilet vomit and spilt Sours shots. The public bench is freezing damp and soaking through my trousers and underwear, into my pelvic bone. I am skeletal.

    The Pride Pin badge is gone. I'm not sure when lost it, or where. Or if I even did. But somehow I trace everything back — the teethy laughs, the dead bonsai, the array of drugs — to that bright, daring object I received six months ago. Even this bench that I'm sat on feels crafted from the same metal, in a way connected to the Pin Badge. It lead me here, swaying from my side. As if the pin itself had been stabbed through my lung all along.

    My numb fingers search for my mother's contact. The birds begin their chirping.

AUTHOR BIOS

Andrea Pinto
andrea.pinto92@gmail.com

Andrea is an MA Creative Writing student at Durham University. She has a background in travel, lifestyle and fashion journalism and has written for the Indian editions of Condé Nast Traveller, GQ, Vogue, Architectural Digest and other publications. In her free time, you can find her exploring the hills (on foot or horseback) or planning her next great adventure in the outdoors.

Catriona Inglis
catrionarji@yahoo.com
Twitter: @catriona_inglis

Catriona writes both prose and poetry and expects to complete her MA in Creative Writing from Durham University in September. Her research interests are in the fields of medical humanities and disability studies, and she hopes to pursue a PhD in the near future. Catriona's writing focusses on depictions of non-normative and disabled bodies, her kinship with her Scottish heritage, and the idiosyncrasies of the rural west midlands where she grew up.

Eden Ward
Edenward.c@outlook.com
Instagram: edenward_writing

Eden Ward is an MA Creative Writing student at Durham University. Her work explores the complexities of girlhood, gender, and love, exploring equally platonic, familial and romantic relationships. Graduating with an LLB in Law from Durham University in 2022, her writing primarily focuses on poetry, with an occasional foray into prose.

Ed Nickols
ed.nickols@sky.com

Ed Nickols is a fiction writer from Lincolnshire. Ed was inspired to get writing after reading George Saunders' 'Tenth of December' wherein he realised stories could be both weird and of literary merit. His current favourite word is 'benthic'. This is his first publication, and he's currently writing a novel.

Elizabeth Marney
lizziemarney@hotmail.com

Elizabeth Marney is a poet from the North West. You can often find her sitting by a river thinking about nature and writing something mildly macabre or unladylike.

Ellie Dyer-Brown
elliedyerbrown@yahoo.com
Twitter: @elliedyerbrown

Ellie Dyer-Brown is a fiction writer from North Yorkshire, pursuing an MA in Creative Writing at Durham University following her BA in English Literature. Growing up with the wild landscape of the moors on her doorstep, she developed an interest in writing about the folklore and mythmaking of isolated communities. She is currently working on a short story collection on this theme set in a fictional Yorkshire town called Bluff. In her spare time, she writes comment articles for Palatinate, Durham's student newspaper.

Izzy Bremner
ibremner@talktalk.net

Izzy Bremner is a Creative Writing MA student at Durham University. She completed her BA in English Literature at Durham in 2022 and undertook her MA to pursue her childhood dream of being a writer. She enjoys drawing people's pets and taking long walks through the countryside in her spare time.

Kate Paterson
kate.paterson2001@gmail.com

Kate Paterson is a fiction writer born in Canada and raised in Shropshire. She is a MA Creative Writing student at Durham University and graduated from Loughborough University with a BA in English with Creative Writing. Kate works with both long and short fiction, through exploring and researching psychological and societal developments of platonic, romantic, and family relations. She also enjoys researching how to rework classics texts, specifically Greek and Latin, in order to fit within modern settings and narratives.

Matthew Ainley
Matt.ainley01@outlook.com
Instagram: @booksheadrevisited

Matthew Ainley is an MA student in Creative Writing at Durham University and achieved a BA in Liberal Arts at Durham University in 2022. He writes both long and short pieces of fiction and is currently working on a longer piece of literary fiction. He has contributed articles and fictional pieces to Palatinate (Durham Student Newspaper) and From the Lighthouse Magazine, of which he is currently Fiction Editor. His writing is inspired by contemporary fiction, and he explores themes ranging from masculinity and sexuality to adolescence, independence, and mental health.

Nupur Mudgal
nupur.mudgal29@gmail.com

Nupur Mudgal is a writer, born and raised in India. Before pursuing MA in Creative Writing at Durham University, she did MA in English from her home country. She has worked previously as a Content Writer for leading brands. She frequently tinkers with poetry styles to spin new tales. When she's not tapping away at her keyboard, she is often found exploring new forms of exercise, from aerial yoga to underwater basket weaving (okay, maybe not that last one).

Paul Haswell
paul.haswell01@gmail.com

Paul Haswell is a writer from the Peak District who studied an English BA at Durham before completing his MA in Creative Writing. He writes short stories and occasional poems that most often bring together the surreal and the real. He loves comedy in all its forms, whether it's literature, TV or film. Outside of writing he is a lover of the outdoors and animals; he is happiest hiking and camping in the Lakes or the Peaks.

PENINSULA

2023